Melodies Of Heritage And Culture

Aditi Jana

/ BookLeaf
Publishing

India | USA | UK

Made with ❤ on the BookLeaf Publishing Platform
www.bookleafpub.in
www.bookleafpub.com

Dedication

I dedicate the book to my dear parents Amiya Kumar Jana and Kalpana Jana who are everything for me. Thank you.

Preface

I surveyed some places of cultural interests in Purba Medinipur and Paschim Medinipur. The places bear a rich connection to the legacy of Bengali heritage, tradition and rituals. Purba Medinipur has contributed greatly to the Indian independence movement. My poems bear some reflections of our effort in shaping the history of Indian independence. Some of the poems are on popular Bengali folk tales. The poems are all about the rural, local flavour of both the districts of Midnapore. These are all about our cultural roots. I wanted to document the rich tradition and heritage of my place. That's why I have chosen the space of poetry. I would be very happy if my small initiative can bring positive changes in society by helping Purba Medinipur in getting a G.I. tag for our cultural practice of Goyna Bori, by getting digital archives of Nimtauri Smritisaudha and the female martyr Matangini Hazra's house and museum, and by ensuring the veteran artist's pension for Pushpa Rani Jana of Sabang who received the National Award as a first madurkathi- artist decades ago.

Acknowledgements

I am grateful to my parents who have always encouraged me to create something new. I am grateful to all my teachers. I am grateful to all the 4th SEM students of English department of my college i.e. Shahid Matangini Hazra Government General Degree College for Women, who have just completed an internship project on cultural studies under my supervision. They have supplied me with informations about many unknown facts of Purba Medinipur. I am grateful to my elder brother Arun Prakash Jana and my younger sister Ananya Jana who have immensely helped me in being creative and innovative in every possible way. Thank you.

1. In Nimtauri Smritisaudha

A wonderful storehouse you are.
A gallery of paintings you are.
You remind me how
Purba Midnapore's cultural past lies there.

A harmonium of Mukundaram
Stares at visitors with the unheard tales
Of cheering the revolutionaries.

A chair of Birendranath Sasmal
Still waits for meeting the anti-colonialists.
In the midst of a book-packed library.

In Nimtauri Smritisaudha
The colonial memories
Of Indian Independence Movement
Are still kept alive.
The unsung heroes
Still wait for you there
To breathe into you
The indomitable courage of Purba Midnapore.

1. On meeting Sabek Chitrakar

In a busy retreat from the Patachitra Village
Of Naya I suddenly met a woman artisan.
Sabek Chitrakar is her name. The lady came
Forward to invite me to her painter's world.
My eyes got charmed with the Indigenous
Lifestyle painted on her folk artifacts. Holding
Three tea trays she explained the oral tales of
Sowing , reaping and harvesting the land that
Lay behind the painting of the three pictures.
My mind leapt up in joy to salute this ordinary
Woman of extraordinary perception. *Sanjher
belay jamunar jol* was her next gift to me. My
Mind flew to the land of Vrindaban, to the land
Of eternal lover Krishna and his beloved Radha.
An eternal lease of life to oral storytelling culture
Is granted thus in *patuas'* colours. Folk paintings
Of a rural lady transform into a çultural mapping.
Look! An artist's coloured mind in *Macher biye,
Pakhir biye* restored Bengali culture from fading.

2. Goyna Bori

Edible Jewels of the kitchen
Are spread over the roof.
The women are preparing the dumplings.
The earrings, the crown and the necklace -
All designs you can find in them.
Purba Medinipur's women
Preserve the heritage in them
With so much care and love
To remind the future generations
Of their sustainable world.

3. Lausen

The valiant man on a horse
With a sword in his hand
Stares at the visitors in Moyna garh.
He is the valiant Lausen,
The fearless one in *Dharmamangal*.
He is the one who made the sun
Rise in the west, thus the myths run.
Moyna Garh, the place of illuminating Rash fair,
Moyna Garh , the place of an island- palace
Is whispering the unknown tales from history.
The zamindari remains an epitome of mystery.

4. Lost in Folk Magic

Patachitra gram, the folk village of Midnapore
Bejeweled with scroll painting and oral songs
Stands amidst organic colours and sends
Messages of sustainable development goals.
Manasamangal, Chandimangal, Ramer Banabas
Sung by patuas are all about Bengal's culture.
Art, heritage and tradition all blended together
Reveal Bengal in its peerless folk- splendour.

5. Visiting Matangini Hazra's House

Matangini Hazra, the aged woman holding
A tricolour flag in her hands and marking
The victory of an unyielding spirit is lying
Dead on the ground with blood oozing out of her
Bullet-shot breast. Matangini Hazra, our
Septuagenarian martyr who empowered us
Lived in this two-storied house of Alinan once.
The wildfire of revolution settled here. You'll find
The rebellious mother of Quit India with a flag
And a triumphant conch in her hands.
That very hut and the museum of Matangini
Being very cradle of colonial past of India
Deserve much care and preservation.

6. A Tribute to Sushila Samanta

Soyadighi village of Medinipur
Nurtured a great mother
Named Sushila Samanta.
Notice the horrifyfying painting in *Smritisaudha*
Of Nimtauri! The wife of Prabhas Samanta
Fights with the Englishmen in her patient
Grace by not disclosing the hiding place
Of the revolutionaries to the policemen
Even when they warn her to throw her child
Into the burning fire. The great mother and
The great daughter of mother India saved
Thus the holy name of our martyrs' land.

8. Chaksudan

An indigenous figure without eyeballs
In a scroll painting waits.
An indigenous figure painted with eyeballs
In the next scroll painting stares at the *patua.*
A tribal ritual it is. A tribal faith it is.
Commissioning an artisan to paint
Two eyes in patachitra to give sight
to the dead is still a revered one.
The practice will make his jounery
In afterlife easier. CHAKSUDAN it is.

9. The Uncrowned King of Midnapore

A true son of the soil
Wished thus. A statue
Of Birendranath Sasmal
With his head held high
Stands in Kaloi field.
The supporter of Swadeshi
Movement never let his
Head bow down
In his lifetime. *Deshapran*
He was. The soul of the nation
Desired a unique cremation of his
Lifeless body with his head held
High even after his death.

10. Visiting Bragabhima Temple

The myths of *Dakshajagnya,*
The death of Sati with Shiva's *Tandav,*
Bishnu's *Sudarshan Chakra*
Cutting the lifeless body of Sati, and
The very fall of her sacred parts
Have given birth to *Shaktipeethas* thus.
So many beliefs, So many rituals,
Revolve around the deity of ours.
The temple of Bargabhima
Standing amidst Tamralipta
Has endured the test of time.
The divine Mother there
Rests in power and
Protects her followers.
Red hibiscus, *Sindoor* and prayer
Offered to Bargabhima mother
Can help you overcome your evil days.
Visit our temple and utter your prayer.
The mother will surely help you prosper.

11. Prayer for Pushpa Rani Jana

The lady received the National award
Decades ago. The masland artist
Made the whole of Sabang honoured.
The 70- year- old elderly woman
 Needs your Care and protection.

With a superb artistry
Of weaving *madurkathi*
She made the nation
Proud again and again.

Let's stand by her
To arrange for her
The veteran Artist's pension.

12. Bhimpuja

Our Bhima resides here.
Our Bhima waits for you here,
In Kulberia of Purba Medinipur.
On *Bhima Ekadashi* the rural folk here
Assemble before his grand idol to offer prayer.

So many small idols you can find there.
People gift those to Bhima for his favour.

Our Bhima,
The magnificent and the benevolent one,
The powerful and the compassionate one,
Listens to our prayers with his eager ears.
That is our belief. The mighty Bhima in his
Grand image meets all the devotees pious
On the auspicious day of *Bhimpuja*. A couple
Childless can beget a child. The unfortunate
One can overcome his crisis. Expect a miracle
Only for the power of Bhima. Our faith in him
Nurtures our love for him. Come to our Bhima
With food, flowers, devotion and offer your prayers.

13. Moyna Model

Can you name
An aquaculture
Practising area
In Midnapore?
It is our Moyna,
The home of
Thousands of
Fish cultivating
People.

A prospering community
With their Moyna Model
Is setting new records of
Economic sustainability.

Moyna Fishery Model
Is a process of bonding
The global and the local.

Thousdnds acres of land
Are converting into water
To boost their heritage of aquaculture.

14. The Owl of Lakshmi

Lakshmipencha, the owl of Lakshmi
Is draped in colours of plenty
In a patachitra of *Patua community.*

Red for the wings, yellow for the body,
With orange in legs and beak,
The owl looks stunningly steady.

Lakshmipencha, the carrier of Mother Lakshmi
And the emblem of Bengali affluence and bounty
Repeated its journey in Bengal's cultural legacy
Of patachitra painting to prove Bengali identity.

15. Conch of Victory

A conch in a museum of Alinan
Is safely kept. A conch of veteran
Matangini Hazra is for her devotion
To a noblest cause. It's an indication
Of the victory of the colonised on an
Imperialistic discourse.

16. Visiting Bhowmik Para

Bhowmik Para, a small area near Chanserpur
Is full of the women- artisans of Medinipur.
The expert female hands there do wonders
By designing jewels of the kitchen. Curators
Marvellous bring the tradition of jewel wearing
and eating. *Goyna Bori,* Bengal's heritage fixing
An identity for the rural women requires a GI tag.
Women artists of Purba Medinipur should bag
A status of Geographical Indicator for dumplings
Of *biuli daal.*Jewels make women beautiful. Does
Not this art of cultural practice make our women
More glorious? Surely it does.The warmth of love
And affection, attention and association weave
An intangible heritage of *Goyna Bori* of ours.

17. Jagannath Temple at Digha

With a pomp of splendour
And a divinity of the soul
People kept you there.
Lord Jagannath at Digha
Along with brother Balaram
And sister Subhadra waits
For the devotees since
Auspicious *Akshyaytritiya*.
The temple built reminds
One of Puri's Jagannath temple.
Hail Jagannath! The protector
Of the world, rest in my soul.
Let my soul be your temple.
Let our truth be your temple.
Let me start an intrapersonal
Communication to reach you.

18. Rash Fair of Moyna

Rashmela, the heritage of our district
Rashmela, the belief of Purba Medinipur
Rashmela , the ritual of Purba Medinipur
Confirming our Bengali identity invites
Millions of people to this sacred site.
Having a bath on the holy *Rash Purnima*
Lord Krishna, the *kuldevta* of Moyna palace
Journeys by boat on the lake surrounding
The palace along with His two consorts.
People flock the grand journey.The burning
Of the incense, the enkindled lamps, *kadma,*
The *Harinaam sankirtana* endow a strange
Grandeur here. A peace of mind is restored.

19. Dejection

Alone on a tiny space,
Alone in a lonely noon
I weave my thoughts.
No solution. No conclusion.
Agonies swell in my heart.
A migratory bird enters into
My garden leaving the worries
In a far away land.
"Bird! Will You fix me
On your wings and
Let me roam with you in a
Stress-relieving space?" said I.
"I come From myths. I live in folk tales.
Let's hover in the land where
The marriage of birds is done."
The bird replied.
My mind recovers the memories
Garnered in folk village of Naya.

20. Journey by a Boat

A boat loaded with people
Is carved on Shiva temple
In red bricks of terracotta style.

The ruined palace of Lausen
Unfolds the myth of the lake.
Lord Biswakarma's massive power
Built deep girdles of water
Surrounding the land of the emperor.

No intruder will find a safe access
To the land of Moyna Garh's king.
He must board on a boat to cross
The water full of snakes, crocodiles.
That was the belief and also a myth.

The journey by a boat on the days of
Holy *Rash Purnima* puts on a magical
Look. Thousands of pilgrims eager of
Krishna's boating with consorts palpable
Flock on the holy land of Moyna Garh.

21. A Bruised Mind

I need a reliever or a painkiller.

A mind injured,
A mind bruised
Needs some healing.

A woman alone-
A woman deserted
Needs some comfort.

The act of humiliating someone
Is the sprinkling of a little acid
On someone. It burns. The soul
Cries out. But the pain remains unheard.

Let the bruised soul fly high
To a terrain unknown.Let the soul
Kiss some magical elixir. Let it
Wake up with some unknown folktale
Where miracles happen and Gods roam.
Let it meet some deus ex machina to forget
The burns and take a stance to renew its self.

22. Echoes in Nimtauri Smritisaudha

You, the silent spectator of the relentless time!
You, the witness of the glory of martyrdom!
You, the recorder of our struggle for freedom!
You, the heritage of Purba Medinipur! You speak
To us through words, books, records, images.
The echoes of the images unfurling lots of tales
Of Sushil Dhara, Ajay Mukherjee, Birendranath
Sasmal and the great women of Purba Medinipur
Seem enchanting. Every drop of blood I feel.
Each cry I hear. I take a deep thrilling plunge
In your pool of memories. The paintings speak
Of my cultural roots to restore me in the present.

23. Khirai Valley

The flowers await you.
The flowers amaze you
With their splendid queues.
The floral space on a bit of land
Shall remind all of a beautiful heaven withal.

Khiral flower valley, the place in Panskura,
Famous for its scenic magic and lovely forms
Will mesmerize you with an appeal irresistible.

24. The Heroes

Oh mother! Where are your sons gone?
Have you counted their number? All gone
For your sake, mother! All died to achieve
A noble cause. All were born to sacrifice
Themselves to your altar, mother! Departed
Brave hearts of Purba Medinipur! Return to
Your Mother once again and let your courage,
Passion and enthusiasm fill her treasure trove.
Our mother needs her patriots now. A nation
Needs to be built anew with the memories of
All departed unsung heroes. Hear! This bleak
Hour cries for a liberation from hypocrisy and
tyranny. Glorify India again with your noble ideals.
Gunamani Hutait, Paran Chandra Mondal, Jeevan
Krishna Santra, Upendra Nath Jana, Pratap
Chandra Ghanti, Ajit Maity, Fanindra Nath Bera,
Makhan Bala Das, Manindra Nath Parua,
Haragobinda Samanta, Radha Nath Jana,
Rajendra Nath Manna, Gajendra Nath Das, Purna
Chandra Maity, Hiralal Dhara, Sanyasi Charan Kar,
 Rakhal Chandra Samanta, Haripada Das, Basanta
Kumar Hazra, Kishori Mohan Hazra, Kishori Bala
Adhikari,
Rasamoy Khatua, Basudeb Maity, Mahendra Nath Dolui -

All fought for your lofty cause. The names are shining
Bright in *Smritisaudha* of Nimtauri. Oh! The lion-hearted
People, rise you all! Ignite your holy spark in us.

25. Goddess Jhingleswari

She loves sea-crabs.
A non-vegetarian deity
Of Bhabanipur Village
In Nandakumar, listens
To our problems and grants our wishes.

Mother Jhingleswari,
The powerful deity resides in a temple
Built on a mast. A river ran by the temple
Once. It's a belief. The freedom fighters
Took shelter there. People believe so.
The Mother protects her children. We think so.
Janmastami, Durgotsav are the festivals grand
When devotees flock around this divine Mother.
Keep a *mannat* with your purity and call Mother.

www.ingramcontent.com/pod-product-compliance
Lightning Source LLC
Chambersburg PA
CBHW051001030426
42339CB00007B/423